More Than
Words

Lauren Kramer

Order this book online at www.trafford.com
or email orders@trafford.com

Most Trafford titles are also available at major online book retailers.

Printed in Victoria, BC, Canada.

ISBN: 978-1-4269-3389-9 (soft)
ISBN: 978-1-4269-3424-7 (ebook)

*Our mission is to efficiently provide the world's finest, most comprehensive
book publishing service, enabling every author to experience success.
To find out how to publish your book, your way, and have it available
worldwide, visit us online at www.trafford.com*

Trafford rev. 07/14/2010

Trafford
PUBLISHING® www.trafford.com

North America & international
toll-free: 1 888 232 4444 (USA & Canada)
phone: 250 383 6864 ♦ fax: 812 355 4082

Love
Granted

How Did You Know?

I was walking around, acting like everything was fine.
But you saw right through the act, straight to this heart of mine.
Not even my own boyfriend could tell
All of the pain and the secrets that I kept well.
I was on lock, but you found the key.
Did not think that anyone would find me.

Thought it might have been written on my head.
But you looked a little deeper instead.
When we spoke; you would stare deep into my eyes.
And did those things that made me realize.
That you know me better than anyone can.
It is almost like it was part of God's plan.

How did you know?
Just what to do?
All the love that you show
I cannot believe you broke through.
Reaching right into my soul.
And knowing everything that is there.
You are the one that makes me whole.
How did you know how to care?
How did you know?

Kisses to the Clock

Time flies when you are having fun.
But with us, it seems to always run.
The minute you come to my door
We end up back there once more.
And no matter how we try to make it last
Everything just goes so fast.

I know it sounds silly and strange
To think that what I do could make time change.
But that does not mean that I would not try
To stop the time from slipping by.
Like an hour glass full of sand
I need to make you understand.
Just how much our time together means to me.
I have got a funny feeling you are my destiny.

I blow kisses to the clock
Hoping somehow that time will stop.
Because all I want to do
Is be right here with you.
And make every moment that we are together
Go by slowly and last forever.
That is why I blow kisses to the clock.

Rose

The taste of your kiss is as sweet as the scent
Of a summer rose that has been heaven sent.
To feel your lips so tender
Like the delicate petals, I surrender.
Reaching to you like a flower toward the sun.
In my heart, I know you are the one.

Like petals capturing the rain
You have absorbed all of my pain.
Making me feel brand new.
I am protected by you.

Your love is like a rose
Getting more beautiful as it grows.
It is so wonderful to see
The precious love surrounding me.
It is strong, never frail.
I know that we will prevail.
This my heart knows
Because your love is like a rose.

Whisper

When you brush my hair aside
And gently touch my face
My feelings I cannot hide.
There is no better place
Than right here with you.
You make my dreams come true.

Whisper sweet words to me.
Get as close as we can be.
Hold me in the dark, silent night.
And when the moment is just right
Whisper.

All My Life

You are so much more than I deserve
Because you are perfect in every way.
You love me and every curve.
You always have sweet words to say.
Even when I get angry
Or do not feel like a beauty queen.
You still seem to love me
And make my life a movie scene.

You know me better than my closest girlfriend
And say the words that I was thinking.
You can even see the things that I pretend.
At times, it does not seem to sink in
That you and I are truly one
Not just in soul, but in mind.
Our love will never be undone.
A better person I could not hope to find.

I have been waiting for you all my life
Praying for this day
When you would see my strife
And take it all away.
Now I cannot believe that you are here
Standing next to me
Wiping away every tear
Filling me with serenity.
I have been waiting for you all my life.

Fugitive

The lights are flashing red and blue
But I keep on running ahead.
In the opposite direction of you.
Away from the words you said.
And I do not know where I am going
Because you have thrown me off track.
With the feeling that keeps growing
And makes me want to turn back.

Once you said, "I love you,"
I heard the siren wail.
But after what I have been through
My heart has become so frail.
Scared to face more pain.
But still wanting to stay.
I do not want that chain.
So, I start to run away.

Without your love, I just cannot seem to live
But, I am scared, so I run like a fugitive.
Even though you are the one I have wanted.
My old memories leave me haunted.
And I have to flee and hide
To protect the heart inside.
Because the love you give
Keeps me running like a fugitive.

First Kiss

I love the way you moved in slow.
Took your time to get it right.
My excitement started to grow
When you took me home that night.
Another date had ended well.
I could feel we were becoming more.
You felt the same and I could tell
There was something you were trying for.

You took my hand
Then I closed my eyes.
No one had planned
Your beautiful surprise.
I felt our lips brush.
Nothing is better than this
The following rush
Of sharing our first kiss.

We slowly pulled away
Then you smiled and said, "Good night."
I wanted you to stay.
I cannot believe you were so polite.
So, I watched your car drive down the street
Re-living the sweet memory.
I cannot wait until our lips next meet
And you will be right here with me.

Love Denied

Cold

When we were together
We always had sunny weather.
The light would dance upon our skin
As you would slowly take me in
To your arms and sweet embrace.
And I would see that beautiful smile on your face.
But suddenly, the clouds came into view.
Then you said that our love was through.

The fire that we had, I never thought would die.
Cannot believe you said that your feelings were all a lie.
Now the flame that used to burn so bright
Has left my world dark without its light.
It is like my heart has begun to freeze.
You have got me down on my knees
Trying to think of how to make it better
But I cannot warm my soul with another sweater.

What you said before you took the heat away
Left me in the cold.
Do not want to face another day
Because now you are not here to hold.
I do not think I will ever feel the sun
Even though it is shining above.
I really thought you were the one.
It is so cold without your love.

Feels Like

We are a couple, or so they say.
But lately, you have taken your love away.
You never call me like you used to do.
We would always talk for an hour or two.
Now suddenly, I find I am all alone.
Even when we talk on the phone.
Because all I seem to get is dead air.
It is just like you do not care.

The words that you would say.
Used to take my breath away.
But now, they drop like acid rain.
Causing me nothing but hurt and pain.
And when you come over at night
All you want to do is fight.
I can no longer pretend
Because I am staring at the end.

And it feels like
We are already broken up.
Like we are worlds apart
And I am no longer in your heart.
Like the people who we used to be
Are just a faded memory.
That is what it feels like
What it feels like to me.

Ghost

When ever you are not near
I am lost in seclusion.
But even when you are here
It seems like an illusion.
Like your heart is some where miles away.
I just do not understand
How you speak, but have nothing to say.
It is not what we had planned.

I try to hold on
To keep loving you.
But you are already gone.
My arms fall straight through.
All I am left with is air.
And the pieces of my broken heart.
It is like you do not even care
That we are slowly falling apart.

You are just a ghost.
You never stay with me.
I am left alone in the night
With nothing but tears and fright.
There is always somewhere else for you to be.
Knowing that the person I love the most
Is a ghost.

Rewind

It is too late to take it back.
The wheels are set in motion.
The train is leaving the track
And my stomach is rolling like the ocean.
Because I never thought
That you would leave
Because even though we fought
In us, I did believe.

I knew I should not have said it.
But I could not keep it in.
To you, it was the biggest hit
The deepest cut upon your skin.
And I still do not know how
I let it get this far
Because it is something that I would not allow
And now you are driving away in your car.

I wish that I could rewind
And have another try.
I cannot get you off my mind
And all I do is cry.
Do not let this be the end
Of our soundtrack.
I am not asking you to pretend.
Please, let us rewind this back.

Should Be Me

You kissed your girlfriend goodbye.
All I could do was watch and cry.
Thinking it should be me instead of her.
Now as my vision starts to blur
The tears fall from my eyes.
I wonder if you realize
What this is doing to my heart.
It is tearing me apart.

I lie awake.
It is too much to take
Thinking of you.
I do not know what to do.
I cannot keep living life this way.
I am slowly dying more each day
And you do not even know
How much I love you so.
You have got someone else in your heart and head
So, I guess I will just toss and turn in my bed.

It should be me
That you hold tight.
It should be me
In your dreams at night.
The one who gets all your love.
The only one you are thinking of.
Cannot you see?
It should be me.

Stupid Tears

I could tell where the conversation was headed.
I tried to cut it off at the pass.
But then you said the things I dreaded
And things blew up fast.
I started yelling
Then you got in my face.
Where it would go, there was no telling.
That is when the tears began to race.

Like rain drops, they just keep coming down.
I can tell my make-up is running.
I feel like I am going to drown
Because it is me that you are shunning.
And I know
I should not let it get the best of me.
Do not want it to show
Or let the whole world see.

Here come the stupid tears
Running down my face like before.
A compilation of my pain and fears
That I cannot contain anymore.
And I wish that I could hold them back
Because this is just a waste of time.
Do not want to go down that track.
The victim of another love crime
But here come the stupid tears.

What About Me?

Tell me why I am here again
Sitting all alone?
Trying to remember when
This house felt like a home.
Now all that is left is empty space
That I keep on trying to fill.
Because you are always at your work place
And I am here missing you still.

Every time I hear that phone ring
I already know what you will say
Because it is always the same thing.
You are stuck and cannot get away.
It seems like you care more about everyone else.
You make others the priority.
But you never think about yourself
Or factor in the component of me.

What about me?
What about us?
All the things you said you would be?
Where is all the love and trust?
Because it seems that you have forgotten about
The new life you are trying to lead.
Leaving me to wonder and doubt
If from this prison, I will be freed.
What about me?

Where Did We Go?

We do not laugh much now-a-days.
Except when I think of our foolish ways.
And I smile.
I have not seen that version of ourselves in quite a while.
But I am not sure just what to do
Because you love me and I love you.
Still, I miss that light
That shone through us when everything was alright.

You seem to be so frustrated
Like your heart has been confiscated.
You have given way to the darkness and sadness.
Trading our love for this madness.
Back and forth, a fighting game.
But, it does not feel the same.
While I am pretty sure the real you is still there
I just need a sign to show you care.

Where did we go?
Right or wrong.
I would like to know.
How we should get along.
Can we find our way ever?
On this crazy ride.
And stick it out together.
Here side by side.
I just have to know.
Where did we go?

So Wrong

We had it all
Or so it seemed.
Never thought we would fall
Or lose the fantasies we dreamed.
We had the kind of love
That weathered every storm
And other were jealous of
Our light that kept us warm.
Then like the changing of the tide
Everything shifted.
Feels like a hurricane inside
Or a spell that cannot be lifted.

I do not know why we did not see
That this was coming down the line.
Together forever, we would not be.
We tried to think that everything was fine.
But more and more
Our differences were coming through.
We kept inching toward the door.
We were doing the best that we could do.
But the way things blew up suddenly
Really did surprise.
All the words you said to me
Brought tears to my eyes.

How did things go so wrong
When everything felt so right?
Why did we think we were strong
When we could not even see the light?
I cannot believe it has come down to this
There is no beginning, just an end.
So much for never ending bliss.
There is no need to pretend
Because things have gone so wrong.

Back in Love With You

The day you left, my heart broke in two
And you took the other half with you.
I begged you to stay
But you went on your way.
As you walked out the door
I felt all my tears pour.

As I look back on what we used to be
I still do not understand why you are not here with me.
Did I care too much?
Or was the feeling too intense with every touch?
I really need to know
Because I still love you so.

What did I do?
Tell me, what did I say
To make you turn around and walk away?
Why did you go?
I really need to know
Because this feeling is eating me inside
To have my love for you be denied.
Everyday, I wonder if there is something I can do
So that I can be back in love with you.

To Stop Loving You

You called me and asked if I could put my feelings aside
And I could have said yes to save my pride.
But I cannot change how I feel toward you
Because that is what I was born to do.

Even though you say you do not love me anymore
I still love you like never before.
And I really do know
That I should give it up, but, I cannot let go.

To stop loving you is like asking me not to breathe.
It is something that I just cannot conceive.
Like telling the sun not to rise or the wind not to blow.
I will love you wherever you go.
It is something that I cannot control.
I feel it in the depths of my soul.
It is like asking the stars not to shine.
I will always want you to be mine.

Ready to Go, But Not Ready to Leave

My bags are packed by the front door.
I will soon be on my way.
Even though I have done this before
I always seem to stay.
But I am tired of watching my dreams die
Fading out like a shadow.
I cannot find the reason why
I do not feel ready to let go.

I just keep staring down the hall
Second guessing myself.
Hoping that I will hear you call
When you see my ring on the shelf.
But all I hear is the porch door slam
As I close off what could be.
Trying to figure out who I am
And what it means to be free.

I am ready to go
But I am not ready to leave.
My heart does not know
That in us, it cannot believe.
It just keeps holding on
To every memory.
Our love has long since gone.
That is the reality.
So, I am ready to go
But not ready to leave.

Rain

Here it comes again.
I slowly close my eyes and remember when
I had everything that my heart could desire.
But the rain put out love's precious fire.
Now all that I can do
Is watch the rain and think of you.

As I listen to the sound
Of the drops hitting the ground
I dream of a true love that can never be.
And wonder why you are not here with me.
The emotions keep on coming back no matter how hard I try.
Quietly, I lay my head down and cry.

Rain, rain.
Falling gently on my window pane.
Releasing memories from the past.
How they can fade so fast.
With every single drop
I tell myself to stop
Thinking of what we had.
Rain can be beautiful but, oh, so sad.
And someday, I will be able to forget.
But until then, I will stay wet.

Together Again

You have got my number in your phone
But you still sit there all alone.
And I know that you will never call me.
It is just another love and lost story
Because every time you try to dial
You cannot deny, it makes you smile.
But you are afraid to hear my voice
Because you have already made your choice.

You still remember my address.
Yes, you know the street.
I thought that you would care less
Since you admitted our defeat.
But I know occasionally,
Your hand wants to turn the wheel
When ever you think of me
That is when you begin to feel.

Together again.
I know you think about it now and then.
The way we were and still could be
Is now a constant memory.
So, will you take that faithful leap?
Or am I the secret you will always keep?
Do you want to be together again?

Well Gone Dry

When I had you
I thought it was for good.
I did things I was not supposed to.
Did not treat you like I should.
I never thought that you would go away.
Just assumed that you would stay.
But I was wrong.
Now here I sit trying to be strong.

I should have been more careful with your heart
Because my life just is not the same.
Now every day, I am back at start
Since you are not here to call my name.
I am trying to figure out what to do
So that I can be with you.

You do not miss the water
Until your well has gone dry.
And now I know
With every day gone by.
You were the best I ever had.
Cannot believe that I treated you bad.
Guess it makes no sense to cry
Because my well has gone dry.

Sore

Like a bandage, you covered me.
Protected from infection and insecurity.
You kept off the rain
And sheltered me from pain.
But suddenly, you said I did not need you.
I knew exactly what you were going to do.
You took an edge and I held on.
Ripped me off and you were gone.

Now I am exposed.
Everybody knows
Exactly what you did to me.
Broke me open for the world to see.
My heart was wrong
Thinking we were strong.
You do not care about the way I feel.
You did not even give me time to heal.
Like an antiseptic, the feeling burned.
Now, this lesson I have learned.

I am sore.
You hurt me in a way that I have never been hurt before.
You left my heart tender and bruised
While I was hurt and confused.
Ever since you slammed the door
I have been sore.

1,000 Secrets

I thought we had a trusting love
That was made to last.
Something blessed by God above
But that time has past.
Open now are my eyes
To the person that I thought I knew.
Finally, I can see the lies
And the person that is really you.

Like a gate, you guarded them well
And kept them hidden from me.
I was just too naïve to tell
That you wanted to be free.
While my love grew stronger
You were slipping away
Wanting me no longer
By your side to stay.

1,000 secrets is what you kept from me.
You had me living in a false reality.
Believing that our love was true
And that I could trust in you.
Now I cannot forgive or forget
The 1,000 secrets that you have kept.

Love Relinquished

Broken

I never experienced pain like this before.
I gave my all to you, but you still walked out the door.
I finally caught you in your lies
And now I see the truth that is in your eyes
As you try to come up with something new
Basically, I have had enough of you.

My world was once calm and cool.
But now it has turned into a tumultuous pool.
What happened to all the love and trust?
Look at what has become of us.
You left me hurt and abused
When I was so confused.
I thought that you would care
But when I reached for you, you were not there.

My heart is broken
It cannot be fixed.
Heaven and hell have become mixed.
All I can do is sit and cry
Going over all the reasons why
You treated me this way
And expected me to stay.
This time it is over, I know
Because I am letting go.
No words need to be spoken
Because my heart is already broken.

Life Support

I never meant for this to happen.
But I let things go too far.
Now it is beyond fixable.
And I am sure it will leave a scar.
Because when you asked me to be supportive of you.
I did not know you would give me the full weight and all.
And I did everything that I could do.
But now my life has started to fall.

There is always a new problem to bring to my attention.
Even when I try to make time for myself.
You are just trying to get sympathy and affection.
To me, this blow should have never been dealt.
Because I wrapped my world around your heart.
To try to keep you alive.
But while my dreams are falling apart.
You continue to thrive.

I do not want to be your life support.
Do not want to be the air you breath.
Because I just feel like I fall short
And you are choking the life from me.
You have gotten under my skin.
And I cannot let you go.
You are taking all my oxygen.
Now the signs are starting to show.
I cannot be your life support.

The Line

You are sick of me.
I cannot stand you.
We know what it is coming to.
But we are not ready to let it end.
We think we are going to be alright.
Guess it is easier for us to pretend.
Until we have another fight.

I have seen the writing on the wall.
And it looks more like graffiti.
Now I feel ready for the big fall.
So you can say that you do not need me.
Because your heart left long ago.
And there is no use trying.
To play a part in this big show.
You know we would both be lying.

We have crossed the line.
Now we are broken in two.
We will never be fine.
There is nothing more we can do.
Because we have come too far to fix us.
And we both know.
That without love and trust.
There is no where that we can go.
But over the line.

Broken Down

We have run out of gas.
We have reached the end of the road.
There is no way that we can pass
Because we are burning on overload.
Look in the trunk, but you will not find a spare.
There is no patch that can fix us.
We are stuck in the middle of nowhere.

Neither one of us knew
Where we were going.
That is when the whole thing blew.
Now we need towing.
Why did not we ask for directions
When we lost our way?
We played on each other's rejections
And now there is a price to pay.

We have already broken down.
There is no way to turn it around
Because we have used up all our energy.
Trying to save the life of you and me.
But now, it is plain and clear
That there is no love left here.
We have broken down.

Graduated

I always sat at the front of your classroom
Studying your every move.
Trying so hard to catch your attention
I felt like I had something to prove
To try to gain your affection.
Then I got the prize that I fought for
But somehow, it did not measure up
Because no matter what, you always wanted more
Like you were drinking from a half-empty cup.

Studied for all of your tests.
Thought that I could ace your heart.
I tried my very best
But you caused us to fall apart
Taking all the feelings that I had for you
And playing me like a pawn.
That is just not something you should do.
So now, baby, I am gone.

Now, I have graduated
To someone new.
You were over-rated.
With the past, I am through.
The future is in front of me
Shining so bright.
There is so much more for me to see
And the time is right.
I have graduated.

For the Wrong Reasons

I am not dumb.
I know that things are bad.
With every lie you tell, I just get numb
Because it is just not worth being sad.
It is the vicious cycle that we have started
And I know it is killing me
Because for so long, I have been broken-hearted.
I did not see the point in being free.

When I am staring at the unknown
That is when I run back to you.
Not because of the kindness you have shown
But because there is nothing else I can do.
See, I know that this is not right.
Our hearts are not in it anymore.
Still, I do not want to be alone in the night
That is why my mind still is not sure.

I am with you for the wrong reasons.
I am just afraid to let go.
I have been doing this so long
It is become the only thing I know.
I am afraid I am not that strong
To just walk away.
But I do not want to be that weak to stay.
Because I am here for the wrong reasons.

Surrender

We are at our battle stations again
Preparing our defenses.
Both of us are determined to win
But this senseless.
Putting each other in the cross-hair
And aiming our words high.
Treating each other like we do not care
But this time, it is goodbye.

You are wounded, but you keep the fight going
Because you do not want to be a casualty.
You get some fulfillment in knowing
That you are not raising the flag for me.
Because now your pride has taken a hit
But I am not giving in.
I am finally through with it
Your constant need to win.

You put your hands up and walk away
But I do not care if you do not stay.
I will not surrender.
I see your back as a mission completed.
I am not backing down until you are defeated.
I will not surrender.

Here With You

I cannot believe all of the things you said to me.
The words still echo in my head.
I never thought that you would want to be free.
I just cannot put this to bed.
How did we come so far?
Only to wind up standing here.
With me not knowing who you are.
Watching our love disappear.

We have had disagreements before
But now, they just are not the same.
We do not even talk any more.
And you are quick to place the blame.
Suddenly, the love we could not live without
Seems to have lost all meaning.
We no longer lean on trust, but doubt.
And my heart keeps on bleeding.

I am so frustrated.
I cannot take this any more.
It is just more he said/she said
And slamming of the door.
Maybe we should just walk away
Because there is nothing left to do
And I do not really want to stay
Here with you.

Let Me Go

You know how we got here.
I gave you all kinds of signs.
Made my feelings quite clear
But you just kept crossing lines.
Pushing me further to the edge
While you seemed to not care.
And now I am jumping off that ledge
And you say it is not fair.

Do not look so surprised.
You knew it was going to happen.
Now you have realized
That I will not go back to you again.
So, save your words and promises so broken.
There is nothing that can make me stay.
Lies are all you have ever spoken.
Just get out of my way.

Let me go.
There is no saving us.
It is something we both know
So, why make a fuss?
Just let me leave gracefully.
Take your life and move on.
There is nothing here left to see
Because our love is far gone.
Just let me go.

Will Not Be Missed

How did our love come to this
With my ring on the floor?
I turn away from your kiss.
I do not want it anymore.
Because I am sick of the tears I shed
Over all the stupid fights.
My heart has already bled
From the many sleepless nights.

I cannot handle your indecision.
I know you will not make up your mind.
I do not want the constant division.
I am tired of feeling left behind
As you try to do this all alone
It is like I do not even have a part.
It is so clear that apart, we have grown.
I am tired of sacrificing my heart.

There is nothing left to say
Because it is already been said.
You are just standing in my way
And messing with my head.
Making promises that do not come true
For a love that does not exist.
There is no way that we can renew
Something that will not even be missed.